LOVING
OUR
HERITAGE

LOVING

OUR

HERITAGE

TOUCHING THE HEARTS OF THE ELDERLY

PRISCILLA MARTENS
DEANNE RAMSEY

EDGEWATER BOOKS

LIBRARY OF CONGRESS CATALOGING-IN-PUBLICATION DATA
Martens, Priscilla.
Ramsey, Deanne.
Loving our heritage : touching the hearts of the elderly /
Priscilla Martens and Deanne Ramsey.

ISBN 978-0-9792968-1-9
1. Aging—Nonfiction.   2. Elder Care—Nonfiction.
3. Elder Care Assistance—Nonfiction.
I. Title.   II. Loving our heritage.

Published in the United States by

EDGEWATER BOOKS
P.O. Box 13, Buhl, Idaho 83316
www.edgewater-books.com

A portion of the profits of this book are donated to

THE SHAMA FOUNDATION
Providing Opportunity Through Education
www.shamafoundation.com

HONOR YOUR FATHER AND YOUR MOTHER,
SO THAT YOU MAY LIVE LONG IN THE LAND
THE LORD YOUR GOD IS GIVING YOU.
EXODUS 20:12

———

For my parents, Donald and Martha Martens, who gave me a priceless heritage.

PRISCILLA

And for my parents, Dean and Patricia Marriage, who helped me understand the importance of both preserving and passing on the love of family.

DEANNE

TABLE OF CONTENTS

FOREWORD

Loving Our Heritage is a book that will touch your heart and inspire you to action. For the past fifteen months two dear friends of mine, Deanne Ramsey and Priscilla Martens, have stepped through the doors of a local assisted living center every Sunday afternoon to bring blessing and companionship to the residents who live there. It all began when Priscilla's mother moved from her home into assisted living. During Priscilla's regular visits to see her mom, she saw that there was a bigger need and immediately took steps to fill it. She enlisted the help of her friend, Deanne, and that is how their

Sunday gatherings began.

Gradually, a sense of community and sincere friendship developed among all the participants. I noticed how Deanne and Priscilla began to speak of their friends at assisted living with such love and genuine care. It became unclear at times just who was really ministering to whom. They were becoming a "family."

I was delighted when Priscilla shared with me that she and Deanne were writing a book about their experiences at assisted living, but it was really more than that. They had caught a bigger vision than just their weekly visits. This vision was to help educate and train others in ways to honor and actively serve the elderly so that they would not feel forgotten or alone.

Loving Our Heritage is the product of that vision and is filled with personal stories, words of wisdom, humor, practical ideas, resources, lesson plans, and other tools to help each of us "step through the door" into the world of our elderly family members, friends, and neighbors. Also included are some helpful tips for those who know someone that is experiencing dementia or Alzheimer's disease.

You are about to embark on a journey sprinkled with laughter, a few tears, and a lot of love. It is a story worth telling and a story well worth reading. But most of all, it is a story worth making your own.

BARBARA ANNEST

PREFACE

Today we are thinking about our 110-year-old friend and the original group of assisted-living residents who inspired this book. We agree that if we could but grow old as graciously as they have, we would be happy. We desire to share our journey with you, our readers. Writing *Loving Our Heritage* has taught us to hope in the future and to grieve without regret. We have grappled with the present and our purpose. We have found and shared inspiration and discovery. We have prepared for our own aging while coming alongside those who are elderly. We now invite you to join our experience of "finding a way in" to the world of assisted living. We hope our experience will become yours.

Thank you to Barbara Annest for capturing the heart and mind of this book in the Foreword, Lynette Croner for contributing insights on how to reach the elderly with dementia and Alzheimer's disease, Jennifer Helmer and Allegra Koehler for encouraging and helpful feedback on the manuscript, Shannon Corpron for her editing and other technical skills that brought this book to completion, and Edgewater Books for publishing *Loving Our Heritage.*

Very special thanks to Tracy and all the staff at assisted living for caring for our heritage every day.

DEANNE RAMSEY
PRISCILLA MARTENS

I.
LOVING OUR HERITAGE

———

PRISCILLA MARTENS

LOVING OUR HERITAGE

I spend three hours every Sunday at an assisted-living facility with people who average ninety-two years of age. The average is skewed somewhat by one resident who is 110 years old and who could keep increasing the average for years to come.

This book is not about the sacrifices that I've made in order to spend a big chunk of my time with the elderly. Nor is it about shaming others into doing the same. On the contrary, I believe that others will want to do the same after reading about my experiences with loving, and loving to serve, our heritage.

How It All Started

My mom entered assisted living a year and a half ago. Providentially, it's the best assisted-living facility west of the Pecos and perhaps east of the Pecos, too, although I'm not familiar with those parts. The motto for the facility is "caring for our heritage," which I have liberally borrowed from for the title of this book.

My mom was the first person to move into the brand new facility. It was a new experience for her going into in a never-before-lived-in home. I announced to everyone else moving in at later dates that my mom was there first—it gave her an elevated status, because the other residents looked to her for information and reassurance. Mom got off to a good start, which was much different than my dad's foray into out-of-home care.

I clearly remember the day that Dad, who died three years before my mom moved into assisted living, was transferred from the hospital to the nursing home. It was a bitterly cold day, and he was left alone for a while in the transfer van with the door open. I got a blanket out of my vehicle and wrapped him up in it. After arriving at the nursing home, he sat in the middle of the huge dining room and was served a lunch with unrecognizable contents. I wanted to cry. The unspoken motto of that facility was "Good luck!" That place was a long way from "caring for our heritage."

At the turn of the millennium, after being gone for twenty-five years, I moved back to the area where I was born and raised. I wanted to spend more time with my elderly parents, and it turned out I had eight years with my dad. Dad was a people-magnet who attracted company and entertained them with storytelling. I especially loved his stories about the old days. One of my favorites was the one about the local cattle rustler who would steal cows and haul them to the stockyard sale where the owners bought them back. My dad and I could laugh for hours about things that no one else even fathomed as being humorous.

My sisters and I spent Thursday after-noons doing cleaning and yard work at my parents' house. Afterwards Dad sometimes asked if I would take him for a ride around the farm. After doing chores I was hot and tired and needing to get back to my own work, but I tried to accommodate his requests whenever possible. I'm so glad that I did. I have such precious memories of driving the back roads and listening to his stories about what had taken place at various sites on the farm. Those eight years with Dad now seem like a truncated period of time. He spent his last nine months in nursing home care, much of that time asking to go back home. But since home was a ninety-year-old farmhouse, there was no way to accommodate his limited mobility. I was relieved that his time living apart from the only home he had ever known was brief.

It was after my dad's death that I discovered my mom does not have a sense of humor.

Learning Love Language

My mom was the youngest of four daughters born into a pastor's family. She grew up under strict rules and raised her own children the same way. Mom saw things in black and white. She kept a spotless house and frowned on whispering and raucous laughter. One of my earliest memories is reciting Scripture verses and catechism to her, and she demanded perfect recall. To this day I think of my mom whenever I memorize anything. I also keep a clean house—even the waste baskets are empty—and I dislike whispering. I think in black and white to the extent that my favorite animals are black and white. How about raucous laughter? Mom still scolds me for laughing too long and too loud.

The night before my dad's funeral service, my brother and I were talking to Mom about what we would say at the service. My mom's counsel: "Don't say any four-letter words, and don't try to be too funny." Sensing that her remarks were directed more at me than at my brother, who is a pastor, I said, "Mom, I promise that I won't say any four-letter words, but I can't promise about not trying to be funny." My entire life I've wanted to be a comedienne.

After the funeral, in the evening when my brother and I dropped her off at her house, Mom said to us, "I'm very proud of what you said today, both of you," and she looked right at me. It was one of the happiest moments of my life.

Since it had become obvious that Mom and I would not be sharing humorous stories and laughing together at them, I had to learn other ways of relating. She loves animals, so I took my three-legged dog, Mo, along when I visited her. Mom adored Mo. Later the assisted living center allowed animals to visit, so I took the dog there occasionally, too. Mom was even more unhappy than I when Mo died while I was on a trip to Australia and New Zealand. Now every week Mom and I look in the newspaper at the pictures of the dogs needing adoption to see if there is a suitable replacement.

For Mom's first Christmas in assisted living, I decided to have a tea party celebration. Tracy, the owner, graciously consented and even bought some nice teacups and saucers for us to use. I furnished cookies with help from a friend and the local bakery. I also bought a hanging ornament for each resident. Then I enlisted two friends to sing Christmas carols. Another resident's daughter designed the invitations, and we sent them out to the family members. We had a good turnout and took pictures of each resident with her family. The best part was that it allowed residents to get acquainted with each other and each other's families.

I make it my business to know the name of every resident and of every family member who visits on a regular basis. I also know the names of many of the staff, although that's more challenging, because they don't wear name-tags, and there has been turnover. Mom sometimes asks me how I know the names of all those people. I tell her that this is where she lives, and I need to know the names of everyone who lives with and works with her.

Getting to know elderly people takes time, and taking time is almost as challenging as the other factor required in getting to know them: listening.

Silence is Golden

I was talking one day to a staff member about my mom, and I asked a question that required an opinion. The staff member replied, "We're doers, not thinkers." I thought about that a lot afterwards. "Doing" is a hallmark of American culture that is best exemplified in our economy, military, and volunteerism. On the other hand, we're not so good at observing, waiting, or listening. All three of these are necessary qualities for loving and serving elderly people. And I learned all of them after Mom moved into assisted living.

Americans are optimistic, so most of us like to think that we're good at observing, waiting, and listening. A few people really are good at it. The rest of us need to learn to do it. Here's how I learned: I never wear a watch when I go to assisted living. I actually know the time, within five minutes, without a watch. But if I'm wearing one, then I want to look at it to verify the time. If I do that at assisted living, the residents catch me looking and think I'm in a hurry to leave them.

There is no time in assisted living, but there is a routine that seldom varies. So the residents don't know the month, day, or time, because it doesn't make a lot of difference to them.

Coming into an elder's world requires leaving our fast pace at the door. That means, among other things, just sitting and observing. Loud talking and sudden movements frighten the residents. I usually make a short remark and wait three minutes or so to see if there is a response.

It takes a lot of waiting to build up trust, and the elderly won't share what's important to them until they trust you. And they won't trust you until they know that you're interested in them and care about them.

For most of us, things can never move too quickly. Not so for the elderly. For instance, many seniors like old TV shows, partly because the screen shots change about every thirty seconds, and they have time to absorb what's happening. Today's television show screen shots change every two seconds, and the elderly often simply cannot follow. They would just as soon watch the pixels, as I've

27

seen my mom do when the TV malfunctions.

It helps me a lot to keep in mind that quick transitions leave out the elderly. I don't know how many times I've started to leave, and Mom or one of the other residents will share something from the heart. I wouldn't trade that for all the time in the world.

Here's a way to test whether or not you're ready to spend time with elderly people. Observe a picture, scenery, or people for ten minutes. See how close you can get to ten minutes without looking at your watch to mark time. Then watch an old movie or TV show, and see if you find that your mind is wandering and you are becoming impatient with the pace, mentally thinking, "Come on!" or "Hurry up!" Finally, go for an entire day without interrupting anyone who is speaking. We frequently don't even realize that we're not listening. Hint: If you're talking, you're not listening.

When you can pass the test, you're ready for your first visit to assisted living.

Passing the Time

My dad was a volunteer chaplain who visited people in the hospital and nursing homes. People would see Dad on the street and stop to thank him for calling on, or praying with, or leading a loved one to the Lord. I still see people today who tell me how much they appreciated my dad's visits. While I would occasionally accompany Dad on his rounds, I viewed it as his retirement mission in life. I never imagined that I would someday share that mission.

So now that we're inside the facility, what do we do? As little as possible! We're still in the observing, waiting, and listening stage. That was more easily accomplished in my mom's situation, because the fifteen other residents did not all arrive at the same time, and I gradually got to know them over a period of time.

To prevent embarrassing or offending any of the residents mentioned here, I have changed their names. Part of the first group I met at assisted living were three women whose names all started with "W," or the

"Dubs" as I referred to them jointly: Wanda, Wilma, and Wynona. I would tease them, "Why are there so many Ws?"

One evening while I was visiting my mom, we heard a loud crash. It barely registered with me, but I learned that night that a loud crash in a facility for the elderly is a crisis. Mom said immediately, "Someone fell." I ran down the hall toward the sound and found Tracy, the owner of the facility, standing outside the entrance to Wanda's room. Wanda had fallen and was partially blocking the door. Tracy talked Wanda into moving far enough away from the door so that staff could get in. Then she told one of the workers to call an ambulance. The staffer came back twice—first to ask for the address and then to ask Wanda's age. I knew the answer to both those questions.

While everyone was waiting for the ambulance, I went back and forth to give my mom periodic updates. The ambulance arrived and hauled Wanda to the hospital where she had surgery for a broken hip and was admitted for several days. I went to visit her in the hospital, and she looked frail and scared. She told me the food was bad.

Wanda was discharged from the hospital to a nursing home. By this time, it was getting close to Christmas. Several of my friends and I went to see Wanda in the nursing home. She looked like death. She said that her room was freezing, so we found an extra blanket and wrapped her up in it. Then I held her cold hands while my friends sang Christmas carols. I cried after we left. I pleaded with God to save Wanda's life, and I begged Tracy every time I saw her to please bring Wanda back to assisted living. And finally, one day, Wanda did return. She was happy to be back, too, and the food in assisted living looked a lot better to her.

These days Wanda is a busy person. She is the go-to resident for knowledge, as not much escapes her notice, and she knows what is going on with both residents and staff. She encourages the residents and has been helping one of them regain her speech. Even at Wanda's age of ninety-two, God has a purpose for her life, and she still has work to do.

Here We Go!

Surveys of nursing homes in which the residents are asked what is most important to them reveal that residents want independence, control, privacy, legacy, normalcy, and spiritual comfort.

Wow! They want the same things that we do! Realizing that the elderly are a lot like the rest of us can go a long way towards helping us relate to them in a meaningful way.

After I had spent several months visiting at assisted living, I began to see a gap that I might help to fill. First, though, I needed assistance. Providentially, many of my friends are teachers, so any gap that required teaching was readily filled—after an appropriate amount of persuasion. Here's where I introduce Deanne, who is a staunch and loyal friend, as well as a teacher. While there were a number of activities for residents during the week, there were no activities on weekends. So I began to talk to Deanne about how we might address some of the residents' needs on weekends. And that was how our three-hour stay on Sundays began. We don't give the time an official name, because we want it to be as inclusive as possible, and labeling creates barriers. The residents don't seem to mind that there is no name, so they each call our time with them different things.

We started with a half-hour test run. Deanne read several stories interspersed with three to four old hymns, since many of the residents were familiar with them. My mom can sing every verse of most Lutheran hymns from memory. Deanne gradually added short, encouraging, spiritual messages, and we closed with prayer. The time also expanded from thirty to forty minutes—given the nature of teachers.

Deanne spends at least three hours in preparation for each Sunday. When I have to substitute for her, I also spend three hours in preparation: two and a half hours praying fervently for ideas, and a half hour on what I will present.

My job on Sundays is to help round up residents, maintain order, inject humor, and sing loudly. You would think that this would be easy to do, but sometimes I'm very busy. If the residents are distressed or feeling ill, they may need to go in and out of the gathering, and most of them are in wheelchairs and require assistance. Sometimes they cough or have a runny nose, so it's good to have water and tissues on hand. I make sure that they have sweaters and blankets, because they feel chilled in our meeting room. Sometimes family members show up to visit, and they either come in and join us, or the resident leaves. Wanda's great-grandson set her phone ringer to rock music, so if she gets a call, we all start rockin' and rollin' until she answers it.

When we first started our Sunday gathering, some of the staff members immediately grasped what we were doing and were cooperative and helpful. Others were uncertain, and a few were openly hostile. That's to be expected. How did the staff know they could trust us to show up, or that our meetings would benefit the residents? Nowadays, however, the staff has everyone in the room by the time we arrive. I said to Deanne, "What if we didn't show up?" And Deanne replied, "They know we'll show up."

On the other hand, the residents never remember that we come on Sundays. They say that they forgot we were coming, or that they thought it was Wednesday, not Sunday, or that it can't be "that time" already. What the residents never forget are the few times that we haven't come because we were out of town. As soon as we reappear, we tell them that we missed them and show them pictures of where we were and what we did. And, if I have to substitute for Deanne, Wanda asks the next Sunday, "Is Deanne coming today?"

Touching Hearts

Our Sunday program time is just the beginning of our three-hour stay. After the meeting, we wheel the residents to their places at the table. We have intentionally backed up our meeting time to their suppertime in order to minimize demands on the staff. Deanne and I bring our own food and eat with the residents, Deanne at one table and me at another. After everyone has finished eating, those who want to, gather at one table to socialize. The conversation generally recalls earlier days, as that is what the residents remember best. We talk about favorite places, animals, pies, children, grandchildren—anything that elicits interest. One night we talked about canyons, and one of the residents went to her room, got her calendar, and proudly showed us a canyon in another state that she had visited.

To spark conversations, Deanne will show pictures on her iPhone of dogs dancing, baby ducklings, small children, and the Rockettes. One of the residents had been to see the Rockettes seven decades before and asked if they were the same dancers. Deanne and I laughed about that afterwards, but we are careful not to demean the residents. I no longer laugh at jokes involving the elderly.

When we're finished socializing, I spend some time with my mom in her room. I want her to feel special and to give her unique attention.

After that, it's time to go home. Deanne and I usually debrief for at least a few minutes, and I'm worn out by the time I get to my house. I eat a sack of popcorn while watching *Masterpiece Theatre* and fall asleep on the couch. But I go to bed happy. What I do at assisted living is the only thing I do that I never have any doubts about.

Caring for Our Heritage

I once attended a big event where I was hoping to meet the coordinator. I knew only her name and had no way of identifying her in a crowd of hundreds of people. Suddenly, the sound system went out. Then one person moved toward the sound controls, and I knew that I had found the coordinator. Whoever is in charge is always responsible for responding first to crises and problems.

The critical component that makes out-of-home care excellent or horrible is the staff. Let's start with the owner. It took me a while to realize that Tracy knows everything that goes on in her facility. She could tell me when I had been there and what I did while I was visiting. Much more importantly, she knows everything about the residents and what they're doing. That's the critical job of an administrator—to know what's going on and to immediately fix things that go wrong.

I don't know what Tracy pays her staff, but it could never be enough. There are two workers per shift, and they do everything that involves the residents' personal needs. In addition, they prepare meals, clean rooms, do laundry, dispense medications, and take care of anything else that needs to be done. They respond instantly when a resident uses the call button, a response that I seldom witnessed when my dad was in the nursing home. My mom never uses the call button, which actually places an extra burden on the staff.

Early on I decided that when I was in the facility, I would do everything possible to help staff members. One evening at suppertime a resident fell, and one of the workers had to take him to the hospital. The other staff member had way too much to do alone, so Deanne and I helped serve the food and clear the tables afterward. Mom said that I was good at that, and maybe I could get a job working there!

When I visit my mom at mid-week, I frequently bring in the mail. I do other things to help out, too, such as fetching items for residents or just talking to them to give staff a break. One evening a resident fell and bled on the carpet, and Deanne and I helped blot up the blood so that it wouldn't stain.

Because the staff at my mom's facility do a good job, I want to show them honor and appreciation. I give them a card on holidays and a gift, usually candy. I thank them when they do something for my mom and when I leave the building.

I ask permission from staff for whatever I do while in the facility. One time I did not, and that was the only time I did something that resulted in a problem.

Of course, there are differences of opinion among the caregivers of an elderly person. If it does become necessary to take an issue up the chain of command, I try to focus on what is best for my mom, not on being right.

The staff are the "representatives" who provide care for our family members. They're caring for our heritage. If it weren't for them, we would be providing the care ourselves. I don't ever want to take them for granted or view them as anything less than equals in partnering to care for my mom.

Presence is the Message

The message that I want my mom and other residents to hear is very simple:

God loves you.

I love you.

I care about you.

I'm here for you.

The majority of the time my presence delivers the message. The elderly residents aren't looking for eloquence. They're simply looking for someone to walk through the door.

I remember when I was young and went to the nursing home to visit my grandmother. Every time I entered, she was watching the door. My mom does the same thing. When residents can't leave, the only hope they have is that someone will arrive. Mom said to me on one visit, "I'm so glad to see someone I know and like!"

I used to think that the elderly were "locked in" to a state of mind and body. Nothing could be further from the truth. At one time they may be confused, irritable, anxious, and demanding to go home. At another time they may be alert, happy, eager to converse, and grateful. Sometimes their state of mind can be linked to a lack of visits from family that they may or may not be able to articulate. Other times residents are tired, not feeling well, or just out of sorts. You know, a lot like us!

The residents who seem the worst off may be the ones who change the most. I've seen elders who had severe strokes go from staring and not speaking to smiling, speaking, and responding. A female resident who spoke only gibberish at first now intermixes her babble with real words. She appeared in the hallway one day while I was knocking on someone's door.

"Hellooooo," she said, "Humsnockwer."

"So, she's not in her room?" I asked.

"Humdonwer," she responded, pointing in the opposite direction.

"Okay, I'll go find her." We both smiled as I left, having enjoyed a normal conversation.

People go into out-of-home care due to lack of mobility, or lack of memory, or both. I encouraged my parents to keep mobile for as long as they could, because their house would not accommodate immobility. And for the elderly who live alone, mobility does not make up for a lack of memory. If an elderly person cannot be trusted to prepare food on a regular basis, to not wander off, and to not otherwise be in harm's way, the only option may be out-of-home care. I think it's sad that memory loss, especially dementia, results in some entering out-of-home care at an early age. In general, for those in assisted living or in a nursing home, there are only two exits: another out-of-home care facility or death.

Because the elderly don't have a way out, we need to find a way in.

Responding in Kind

So, how do the elderly respond when we do find a way in?

There are times when they express gratitude in such a profound manner that it brings tears to my eyes. After our get-togethers at assisted living, one of them will say, "We're so grateful for you," or "There is nothing else like this, and we are thankful that you come," or "I never want to miss this, even though I can't ever remember when it is."

The elderly also express their gratitude by sharing their secrets. At supper one evening, a woman leaned over and said to me, "I have Alzheimer's." I wanted to say, "Right now?" but I just nodded my head and smiled. I don't know to this day if she does or doesn't have Alzheimer's. I don't need to know.

At times the residents give us a hug on the way out, but it's not very often, and I'm careful about touching them. I want to respect their space and their wishes. When I wheel them out to supper and put on their food cloth, I pat them lightly on the shoulder. It's a sign of affection that seems to be universally accepted and appreciated.

I'm not very demonstrative by nature, and I don't say "I love you" very often, not even to my mom. As I said before, my presence carries the message. Mom almost always thanks me for coming and thanks Deanne, too.

If someone is too sick or too tired to attend the get-together, Deanne will go to their room and give them a shortened version of the meeting. The residents are more open to touching when they're sick, frightened, or distressed. If they feel the need, they will grab one of my hands and hold on tight.

Each resident has a different personality. One of them says, "I know him/her" every time Deanne shares a picture. Another person who is musical critiques the singing: the pitch is too high or too low. Still another one has a cynical sense of humor. If I ask if she's tired, she may respond, "Why? Am I bothering you?"

Deanne and I discovered early on that as we helped the residents, they began to do the same for each other. One of them will show another where we are in the song, another will push a person in a wheelchair to the dining room, and yet another will find staff when a friend is in distress. Just because the residents are old and have limited abilities doesn't mean that they can no longer be helpful. Everyone wants to be useful.

Forgetting Being Forgotten

An elderly person in out-of-home care once said to me, "I'm trying to forget that I'm forgotten." She wasn't forgotten, but it's a statement that I've thought a lot about. I don't want elderly people to believe that they're forgotten. Instead, they should be cherished, honored, and remembered. How can we convey that unless we enter their world?

"Well," you may say, "It's good that you spend time with the elderly, but I can't do that. I'm too busy," or "I don't know what to say," or "I may say something stupid or offensive," or "I can't take on anything else." I've said those same things.

I heard indirectly that one of the family

members of an elderly resident refuses to visit her because she calls him by the wrong name. We can't have that! After all, when we were young and couldn't say our parents' names, they ignored us and refused to meet our needs—I think you get the idea. Don't tell me that your elderly relative calls you by the wrong name.

In the past I viewed Sundays as a day of rest and did as little as possible after church. While I never seem to be sick on Sundays, sometimes I don't feel like spending three hours at assisted living. I go anyway, and I always feel better after I do. I have freedom to do what I want every day of the week, but the residents don't. I can eat what I want when I want to—they can't. I can leave my house when I'm bored and want company—assisted-living residents can't. My health is good, and I feel good most of the time—they don't.

It's true that we can't control the circumstances that lead to out-of-home care, we can't control what happens there, and we can't cure people of dying. But just a short time ago, the elderly residents I now see in assisted living were the leaders in their communities. They gave unselfishly and devotedly to bettering themselves, their families, and their community. I consider it a privilege to honor their sacrifice and service by investing a few hours a week spending time with them.

Saying Good-Bye

When my mom first entered assisted living, the next person to arrive was a man who lived on the opposite end of the facility, so I called my mom and him the "book-ends." He was a wonderful person, friendly and gracious to everyone he met. He loved sports and music, and one night at supper he said that he couldn't find his TV remote, and he wanted to watch a ball game. I wheeled my mom to his room, and while I found and fiddled with the remote, he showed Mom a photo book that his granddaughter had put together for him. It was very nicely done, and he was so proud of his granddaughter's work. A few weeks later he died. I went to the visitation at the funeral home where his daughter introduced me to the granddaughter. She was touched when I told her how proud her grandfather had been of the book she had made for him.

This man's death is an example of the best way to leave assisted living. Some people go quickly, while others linger for a long time. It's much easier to accept the deaths than to cope with the other reasons residents have to leave: to go to the hospital or into a nursing home.

Hospitals are wonderful places for saving lives; they're quick, efficient, and discharge people within an incredibly short period of time. Hospitals are also controlling, intrusive, and lack privacy. These last qualities are anathema to the elderly. The residents return from the hospital confused, sick, scared, speechless, and generally dysfunctional. The staff have to do yeoman's work to get them back to normal. Gradually, the residents poke their heads out from under their protective shells and begin to function again. It's wonderful to observe them once more taking an interest in living.

People ask if I get attached to the

residents. Yes, I do, and I take personally what happens to them. It's especially hard for me to handle watching them have to leave assisted living for behavioral or disability reasons. Wilma, for instance, was constantly agitated and wanted to leave the facility. You couldn't go out the door if she was standing near it, because she would try to go out with you. She was often looking for her purse or putting on her coat so that she would be ready to find a ride home. Wilma did laps around the hallways and went into other residents' rooms trying to find her own room. On these excursions she would forget to take her walker and thus had several bad falls. It finally became too much for the staff, and she had to be transferred to another facility.

A few days before Wilma left, the workers were busy, so I spent some time entertaining her. She went fluidly back and forth between talking about events from forty years ago to discussing the current program on TV. She told me to try out her favorite chair by the fireplace, so I did, and I told her it was very comfortable. After a half hour one of the staff came to relieve me. Wilma walked me to the door, hugged me, and then went off happily with the staff member. I cried on the way home. I just could not accept why she had to be moved to another facility.

After Wilma was in her new home for about a month, Deanne and I went to visit her. She proudly showed us around, and we visited for a while in her room. She was markedly less agitated. When we were getting ready to leave, she told us that she knew that she couldn't be a bother to people any more and that she didn't want to be.

Late one night under the cover of darkness, Wilma slipped away to her best and final home. She will never again be confused, frantic, desperate, or inconsolable.

I'm happy for her, but I still miss her.

Being Neighborly

If you've read this far, you may be contemplating the possibility of getting involved with the elderly. But where to begin?

Start by making a list of all the elderly people you know, and decide which ones could most benefit from your presence. Of course, there are your own relatives. But also consider the elderly who are relatives of your friends, those who are your neighbors, and those who are members of your church and civic organizations. Deanne got to know my mom well before Mom entered out-of-home care, as Deanne had occasionally accompanied me on visits and spent holidays with my family. It's much easier to get to know elderly people before they enter out-of-home care. And the elderly who live alone may be just as lonely as those who live in facilities.

All my life I have been blessed to have elderly people living next door. They make the most wonderful neighbors. They all had gardens and were happy to provide tips, vegetables, flowers, and other delightful natural gifts. In return, I helped them lift heavy objects, ran off the neighborhood bullies who frightened them, and checked on them after major storms or power outages.

My current elderly neighbor is very independent. When I check on him while his family is away, I make sure to do it in an unobtrusive way by combining the visit with delivering the mail or the paper or doing other chores. He knows he's being watched, but as long we don't discuss it, he retains his dignity, and I fulfill my neighborly responsibility.

It's sad that Americans have forgotten how to be "neighborly." Jesus said that to love your neighbor is the second greatest commandment, and his most widely known parable describes how to be a neighbor. You'll notice there is no age limit mentioned.

It all boils down to this: How do I want to be treated when I'm old and need assistance? If each of us treats the elderly now in the same way that we want to be treated when we're that age, then we don't need to be concerned about what will happen to us.

You may be wondering how often you should make contact with an elderly person. Here are my guidelines:

1) Something is better than nothing.

2) Regularity is more important than frequency. If you can visit an elderly person

only once a month, go every month at the same time. That way the expectations that you're building will be fulfilled.

3) After you get acquainted, stay longer rather than shorter times. A half-hour visit is fine at the beginning, but gradually extend it to forty-five minutes or an hour. Remember that most elderly people will just be getting ready to engage after a half hour.

4) Increase the frequency of visits as the relationship develops. You'll know when both you and the elderly person are ready for more visits. They will drop hints or even make direct comments. If elders make a point of thanking you profusely for visiting, that's a good indicator that they would like to see more of you.

What about Us?

I'm a Baby Boomer and this book is aimed primarily at Baby Boomers, as it's this generation that has elderly parents.

Many Boomers are sandwiched between caring for elderly parents while also providing care for and spending time with grandchildren. Since it's very difficult to do both, you may decide to choose one at the expense of the other. What I see most frequently is Boomers choosing the grandchild over the elderly parent. That's not only sad for the elderly parent, it's also sad because the Boomer's children and grandchildren may make the same choice some day.

There are times when you cannot avoid having to choose, but on ordinary days here are some ways to resolve the conflict:

1) Take the grandchildren along to visit the elderly. The elderly person will love it, and it's also good for the grandchild to learn how to interact with elderly people. When my dad was in the nursing home, one of his great-grandchildren who visited would often make the long walk from Dad's room to the free soda machine. This took a considerable amount of time, because every resident he encountered along the way wanted to talk to him. Arriving at the machine, he poured a small amount of each kind of soda into the paper cup.

"How does that taste—like gasoline?" I once asked him.

"Mmmmmm, tastes good," he replied, now fortified for the return trip.

2) Stick to a regular schedule when visiting the elderly. That way they are less likely to become frustrated and demanding. If you have to cancel your visit, call and explain. I've had to call my mom a few times to tell her that I couldn't visit because I was sick. I could tell that she was disappointed, but she could at least hear my voice and know that I was thinking about her.

3) Share stories about the elderly with your grandchildren. Let them know when they look or act like your elderly relative. Encourage your grandchildren to honor the elderly by making cards, pictures, or other small gifts. Hang pictures of your grandchildren in your elderly relative's room, and keep them informed of the grandchildren's activities and milestones.

4) Don't criticize the elderly or make jokes about them in the hearing of your grandchildren (or anyone else), unless, of course, you don't mind them doing the same to you when you're old.

Remember what I said about the elderly

in nursing homes valuing independence and control? The following are a few ways to give them what they value:

1) Let them live their own lives. While I do take personally what happens to the elderly at assisted living, I don't try to live their lives for them. Over-identification with an elderly person and trying to control everything that happens has a bad effect on them. It makes the elderly feel helpless, hopeless, and useless. It reduces them to merely existing. It will also wear you out and damage your relationship with others.

2) Let them make mistakes. In the few areas where they are still allowed to make choices, let them choose whatever they want as long as there are not drastic con-sequences. Of course, the problem is that all of us have a different definition of "drastic consequences." My mom has her fingernails painted weekly. I don't think that the nail polish is good for the health of her finger-nails, but she seems to like having it done, so I limit my comments to "That's a nice color."

3) Do what makes the elderly happy. Each time I visit, I bring a bottle of cold water for

my mom. My dad loved cold water and had a small refrigerator in the nursing home for that purpose. My mom grew to appreciate cold water after drinking a lot of warm tap water when she first moved into assisted living. Cold water is a small gift that you can give to any elderly person.

Mom likes to have a lamp that she can reach, so I took her one of my floor lamps, and I keep her supplied with three-way light bulbs. Other residents appreciate newspapers, books, magazines, calendars, or pictures. One caution: Do not bring any food into a facility unless you check first with the staff. For various reasons, there are many dietary restrictions, so don't make any assumptions about what foods are allowed.

4) Do it now. What I would like people to most remember after reading this book is not to delay in engaging with the elderly. Four residents have died in the eighteen months that my mom has been in assisted living. Time is fleeting. I determined that I would have no regrets when my parents died. I had no regrets after my dad died, and I will have no regrets after my mom dies.

I'm investing my time and energy now so that I will be at peace later.

I've heard that assisted living and nursing home facilities will be bursting at the seams as Boomers age. Personally, I think these facilities will be empty except for people with Alzheimer's, at least until a cure is found for that horrible disease. The parents of many Boomers did not make any plans for their old age. They waited until the choice was made for them. I hope that their children and grandchildren won't do that.

Most of the Boomers I know are making plans now. Some of them are building multi-generational compounds. Others are building a small house by their big house so that they can move into the small one and their children will move into the big one. My plan is to build my own assisted-living facility for up to four residents who will share the facility costs and the cost of care. I much prefer to give other people directions than to be told what to do!

Home Again

It's Sunday evening, nearly 6:00 P.M., and I'm sitting at the dining room table at my mom's assisted-living facility.

There is a screeching noise coming from one of the residents as her son appears to massage her neck too roughly. "Stop that!" I say to him. He does, laughing loudly, his voice echoing off the walls as he and his dog leave the building.

The residents are served ice cream with their meal, and everyone cleans their plates. A spoon full of sugar helps... The fastest resident, who eats in under two minutes, gets up too quickly without using his walker and falls. The staff gets him into his chair in front of the TV. Shortly after, I hear his familiar hacking cough and remark, "I think he's feeling better now." Heads nod in agreement.

Deanne is talking gently to a resident who is out of sorts because her daughter is out of town. Before long they are laughing together as the resident tells a story of a bird bathing in a punch bowl shortly before all the guests drink from it. As the story gets passed around, everyone joins in the laughter.

The oldest resident is looking at the book that Deanne read from earlier during our meeting time. She doesn't hear well and likes to read the book for herself after supper—every page.

I fetch a cup of coffee for one of the residents and then hand a tissue to another one. Wanda is coaxing a woman who had a severe stroke to say her name, and suddenly she says it, clear as a bell. We praise both of them.

Deanne shows the residents a video clip of a woman and dog dancing, and then a woman and two dogs dancing. I can tell from the "ooohs" and "aaaahs" when they're viewing the best parts.

I lean back in my chair, enjoying the cadence and the company. I feel contented.

I feel at home.

Epilogue

Mom cratered on Mother's Day. Almost everything in her body stopped functioning except her will to live. Thus began a two-week stay in the hospital in which my mom was up one day, down the next—a constant yo-yo.

Mom will not be returning to assisted living. She will require a full-care nursing home. I told Deanne that it looks like we will be opening up our first franchise.

And so begins the sequel to this book. When Deanne and I told the residents of assisted living that Mom would not be returning, they...

But that's another story for another time.

II.
FINDING MY WAY IN

——

DEANNE RAMSEY

FINDING MY WAY IN

An Early Start

My introduction to caring for an elderly person began as a teenager when my step-grandmother had a stroke at age sixty-one in the late 1950s. She was put in a nursing home; it seemed more like an asylum to me. Chances for her improvement were slim in those days: no therapy, only the basics for making her comfortable. That was my view of standard care at that time. The caregivers were nice enough but very business-like; nothing seemed very personal. Shifts changed regularly, but so did the staff; I rarely saw the same people twice. Grandpa went every day. My family of five visited weekly on Sundays after church, and Grandpa would take us out to dinner afterwards. The sights, sounds, and smells were scary for us kids. We didn't want to go, but my folks wisely took us along anyway. It wasn't easy on them, either. We were aware of my parents' struggles before and after visits, especially my mom's.

These struggles had originated years earlier with Grandma's unforgiveness. Grandma had expected her newly-graduated daughter to open a dress shop with her. Instead, her daughter fell in love with my father, a newly-widowed biologist with a four-year-old daughter—me. They married, and suddenly, I had a mom and a new set of grandparents. When we moved away, Grandma became hard with anger. She disowned her daughter and shunned my dad and me whenever we came back to visit. This caused my grandfather great sorrow, but no one ever crossed Grandma. We were all a little afraid of her. Although Grandpa's attempts at peacemaking failed, he kept in touch with us despite Grandma's hardened heart. When my two half-sisters were born, Grandpa had to love them from afar. My mom's heart was broken because of her mother's unforgiveness. Eventually we moved back to Grandma's hometown. That was when she had her stroke.

Mom worked valiantly to renew her relationship with her mother. Since Grandma couldn't go out of the nursing home, we went to her. When we visited, Mom always took something (mainly us granddaughters) to show Grandma. She sewed bed jackets and pretty nightgowns. We would sit next to Grandma's bed and carry on conversations with her and Grandpa just as though we were around our dinner table. We knew she could hear us, but she could neither speak nor control most movements. She did attempt to respond, and eventually we could make some sense of her unintelligible noises. At first it was very hard for us girls. Over the years it became easier. My younger sisters' antics and stories brought her joy; we knew because she could smile a little on one side of her face.

Somehow we came to know that she understood much more than she was able to express. And somehow we knew she had forgiven my mom and had come to love my dad, my sisters, and me during the five years before she died. Our family had been reunited.

The effects of forgiveness and consistent, unconditional love impressed me. Even more impressive to me was my dad's wholehearted participation in this reconciliation. He forgave his mother-in-law; his forgiveness and my parents' dedication to her care made a huge impact on me. I saw Grandma's heart soften in gratitude toward Mom and Dad in the years following her stroke, and I believe that she finally realized the power of love. Love won, and I resolved to live a forgiving life.

I tell this story to show that in life, relationships count. The older or less capable we become, the more relationships matter. I am grateful to my parents for showing me this at a fairly early age. And as I myself age, this truth has become even clearer. My parents' commitment to my grandma was a wonderful example to my sisters and me. Since then we have participated in the care of several other elderly relatives during their end days, including our own parents. As happens with siblings, we didn't always agree, but we chose to work through any differences because our loved ones' best interests came first. We chose relationship over being right. Sometimes it was hard work, and it was always intentional work, but we did it then and still do it now. As we grow older, we are reaping the fruit of that love, fruit that we see blossoming in our own children and grandchildren.

It is with this background that I came to our local assisted-living facility one Christmas to help put on a program for my friend's mother and other residents. Little did I know that it was the beginning of a new phase in my life.

The Beginning

Priscilla's elderly mother had just moved into an assisted-living center, a beautiful new facility in our little town. It was the third place that owner-manager Tracy had opened in the area. It was nearing Christmas, and Priscilla had plans for a tea party. She enlisted our friend Barbara and me to help her put on a musical program for all the residents. Priscilla organized it; we did the program. Barbara and I were happy to sing together once more; it had been years since we had sung our last program. We enlisted my aunt to accompany us on the piano. All the residents sang with us, enjoying it immensely. There were lovely treats afterwards. It was very rewarding.

To my surprise, I knew at least four other residents besides Priscilla's mother, some through singing in choirs, others through community organizations. Because teaching had completely absorbed my time, I had lost track of these people. It was wonderful to catch up with them.

A few weeks later my organizer friend had a new plan. Would I be willing to meet weekly with the ladies we knew at assisted living, bring them inspirational stories, and maybe even sing old hymns they knew? I agreed to try one Sunday afternoon. The ladies I knew all came, plus a few others. I was impressed that their response was so immediate, so genuine, and so grateful. Priscilla realized early on that a once-in-a-while approach would never work. As busy as I was, I had to wrestle with making a weekly commitment. Eventually I decided that this was a very important work and that I was supposed to be involved. Priscilla was never bothered with indecision about anything. And so it began.

Onward

Over eighteen months our meetings at assisted living turned into something more than stories and hymns. I began seeing what interested each lady. The residents loved stimulation, and although their short-term memory was limited, they had many past memories that they could recall with ease. I knew I could tap into that if I got to know them better. They were always happy to listen, but reluctant to talk.

Knowing that engagement facilitates learning, and since I had a history with some of the residents, I started to include their life experiences in our conversations as often as possible. Soon they were taking part in the conversation and even beginning to contribute spontaneously.

At first I would tell a story and randomly choose a hymn I thought they might know. That moved into telling the stories behind the hymns themselves. Priscilla suggested I read a few children's picture books, since I had so many. The residents were polite listeners at first, but grew to anticipate quality literature. Priscilla was always there with a comment or funny observation, pulling others into the conversation. Once I brought pictures depicting a hymn-writer and his life; the ladies devoured those images. One dear lady announced that she "knew him" (he had lived in the 1700s). Aha! Visuals worked! Sometimes a lady shared an event or experience that directed us to another topic. I leaned on Priscilla's observations and suggestions; another pair of eyes is always valuable. Eventually I began to plan stories, hymns, and visuals around a weekly theme. Children's picture books and funny stories provided a light entrance into weightier topics, all accompanied by as many pictures or actual objects as I could find. At a loss to characterize what we were doing each week when people asked, I would fumble for a word to describe it. One day my former teacher friend and resident, Wynona, referred to us as the ladies "who bring us lessons." "Lessons" it was!

During the past year our topics have included everything from holidays to family to science to fantasy, all designed to stimulate thinking, and often guided by the rich traditions and memories stored away in these ladies' still-curious minds. Because members of our group range in age from their late eighties to 110, there is much historical memory indeed. We became more and more attached to our assisted-living family and looked forward to four o'clock on Sunday afternoons.

At some point we began staying for dinner. In the beginning Priscilla and I carried the conversation. Priscilla sat at one of the four tables, I at another, both of us encouraging the residents to talk. During the winter when it was dark by 5:00 P.M., everyone wanted to head to their rooms immediately after dinner. We visited Priscilla's mom for a while in her room and then took our leave. Later we would comment to each other on how people's attention during dinner always turned immediately to wherever there was laughter and conversation. So we began a new tradition of gathering around one table to visit as soon as the food was gone, inviting all to come.

This brought yet another dimension to our relationships. At first only a few women at one table stayed after dinner, and only one wheeled herself over from another table. But eventually our little "family" grew to five or six. Because of the variety of abilities to communicate, conversation was sometimes difficult, sometimes hilarious. One lady understood all that was said, but like my grandmother, had no language. Nonetheless, she responded to topics with great enthusiasm and perfect rhythm—in gibberish. We would nod, smile, and agree. After a while, however, we even began to understand her. Love transcends language!

Eventually three other residents joined us. Our Sunday afternoons at the facility lengthened with daylight savings time. We saw more energy in the spring, possibly because it stayed light longer, or possibly because over time we had become family. We included anyone in the Sunday after-dinner visit, often laughing together and looking at YouTube videos on my smart-phone.

Time never stands still; we have mourned some deaths already. A few other residents conditions have worsened, necessitating a move to a different facility with a higher level of care. We miss them and try to visit them. At present our group has seven regular attendees. We know our time with these dear ladies is limited, but so is ours on this earth. That makes it more imperative to honor our loved ones fully with what time we have. Sharing life together is the ultimate blessing.

For instance, one Sunday everyone stayed around the table until seven o'clock. When Priscilla's mother finally became tired, Priscilla took her back to her room for a private visit. I also excused myself to join them, as I do every Sunday. That night, however, I felt a little awkward, because three of the ladies had joined us for the first time and didn't know my routine. I worried my leaving would make it seem I was tired of their company. When I excused myself, as if on cue, my 110-year-old friend pushed herself close to me and said loudly in my ear, "I know you. You've just had all of us that you can take!" After laughing at her refreshing directness, I explained that no, I wasn't tired of them; I was going to another resident's room, which was my routine every Sunday. I left chuckling, but knew that I had been gifted with a lesson, and its point was well taken. Regardless of how I view my actions, routine, or motives, if it appears differently to someone else, that's the way it is for them. I learned to prepare the group for my exit without assuming they would remember my routine. Situations like this arise when one is accepted as family. And when you're family, mutual honesty is key.

Remembering...or Not

Over the years I have been aware of the frustration, even pain, of elderly persons lamenting loss of memory and physical function, and experiencing confusion of the present with the past. One day a frustrated resident said to me, "My brain seems to have holes in it!" Some speak of long-dead relatives as though they were just in the next room. One lady wakes up and feels the urge to hurry and fix breakfast for her husband who will be coming in soon from milking the cows. Another says, "I need to call my family. They'll be wondering where I am." You may have heard similar statements from your loved ones whose awareness of the present is slowly slipping away. Memory that robs minds randomly of reality is stressful both to the aging and to those around them.

As I worked with the aging and aged myself, several "why" and "how" questions began to plague me. Why do we forget more as we age? Why do we remember the long ago past better than five minutes ago? There are many books, websites, and support groups for people who want to understand the aging process and how to cope with an aging relative. But how can we actually make a difference in the lives of our loved ones? Are there proven techniques that when used with the elderly produce measurable positive effects on their memory?

A short survey of scientific research quickly revealed these similar findings (italics are mine):

- There is a clear, consistent benefit to cognitive function that is associated with *intellectual stimulation.*[1]*

- "The purpose of activities for people with dementia is not so much restorative, but rather, preventative and enabling. *Activities* are used to reestablish a sense of normal function...a *sense of usefulness, of pleasure*, and to reduce the sense of helplessness and futility these people experience."[2]*

- *Social interaction*, either involving conversation or visitors with a baby

* Refer to Appendix D on page 135 for Works Cited.

or pet, are the most stimulating and engaging activities conferring a positive mood and engaging people for significant periods of time. [3*]

These were the very things that we had discovered. We never outgrow our need for dignity and usefulness. A more exhaustive search might show added benefits, but this is where we began. In summary, science backed up what we had discovered informally. Intellectual stimulation (reading, music, art, engaging past memories), social interaction (relationships), a sense of purpose, and physical activities all have a positive, measurable effect on quality of life. New studies are being planned to examine the role of spirituality in the lives of the elderly. In our work we have discovered that spirituality also impacts residents' quality of life.

On the strength of these findings, we continue to build plans for engaging lessons.

Applying What Works

As our weekly time at assisted living lengthened, both in hours and in months, several patterns began to emerge. As confirmed by research, residents repeatedly responded best to these stimuli:

1. Singing
2. Stories (entertaining, historical, spiritual, informative, scientific)
3. Visuals (pictures, picture books, real objects)
4. Memories specific to residents' histories
5. Personal contact

The most engagement happens when many of the above are used in a single lesson. On those days conversation sparks, and people interact and begin to get to know each other better. In our group a new sense of camaraderie began to grow. Ladies thrown together simply because of their physical or mental limitations slowly became friends. We began to hear prayer requests, observed ladies checking on each other, wheeling each other around, visiting each others' rooms, and taking responsibility in small ways ("She's cold. Could you get her a blanket?" "She's been in her room all day. I visited her after lunch." "She said her name today! I've been working with her.").

My in-residence teacher friend, Wynona, acquired a new mission: encouraging another dear lady, a stroke victim, to talk. She started visiting with her each day, asking her questions, holding her hand. Wynona regaled me with stories about the words this lady was learning to use again. One night after dinner as I left my table for the common visiting table, I invited, as usual, Wynona's "student" to join us. She didn't respond. However, one of the ever-observant employees saw the opportunity and wheeled her over beside her new teacher. For about an hour they sat side by side while Wynona plied her with questions. Wynona's "student" grasped her hand, gazing intently into her face, smiling occasionally. Everyone around the table was smiling and praising them, just as delighted mothers take pleasure in baby coos turning into language. I heard, "Isn't she pretty?" and "Look at that! She smiled!" I could tell Wynona had found a purpose. With those observations serving as ice-breakers, soon conversation was flowing about other topics—just like family. Now Wynona's "student" has joined us for our lessons as well. If you're alive, you have a purpose.

We encourage cognitive growth in the residents by doing these three things: providing short (forty minutes maximum) stimulating lessons, joining them for a meal, and visiting informally, both individually and around a common table. In short, we try to be family, doing what families do, never, however, replacing the residents' own family. In fact, many family members have expressed their appreciation for our efforts.

Not everyone has the time for this kind of commitment, but any part or combination of these make a care center or assisted-living facility a little more like home. I hasten to add that these residents have a great variety of limiting physical and mental disabilities. Some can carry on a lucid conversation; a few have no language. Some have to be fed; others can feed themselves. Some are ambulatory; most are wheelchair bound. Their needs are many and unique, requiring much individualized care. But over time each one has responded to some degree to the stimulations listed on page 80.

Often unappreciated are the many services that able administration and staff provide for their residents. Nursing help, physical therapy, and medical care are all given regularly. The daily caregivers feed, help dress, and keep clean every one of their charges, just like family. Special credit must go to workers for their compassionate and consistent services. What a blessing they are to their beloved residents and their families. Staff members run day and night just managing needs. There is little time for planning extra stimulation.

This is where you, our readers, come in. We've introduced you to the need that exists in facilities everywhere. We've shared the benefits of "finding a way in." Now let's delve a little deeper into the process of creating stimulating lessons.

Choosing a Lesson Focus

Although studying the times and places in which residents grew up will give you some lesson topic ideas, the residents' interests are a great place to start. Relatives can sometimes give clues to those subjects that engage their loved-one's attention. But building relationships with the residents themselves is the best way to discover what their individual interests are.

Through relationship I discovered the ladies in our group

- loved music, especially old hymns (we usually sang a cappella, but they, and all residents, especially responded when someone came and accompanied us on the piano in the main dining room);
- loved history;
- were stimulated by stories about generosity, courage, kindness, animals, interesting lives;
- loved excellent art, whether in children's books, posters, or shown from the Internet;
- were curious about nature (e.g. snowflakes, wild animal recovery),
- loved (and knew) Scripture;
- liked humor;
- loved seeing children, photos of children, or stories about children.

In other words, residents in facilities for

the elderly have multiple interests and talents, just like you and me.

Things to try for variety are

- periodic hymn-singing only with accompaniment, no program or particular theme;
- bringing in school children for a short presentation, songs, or skit;
- asking local piano teachers for students who might like to perform;
- asking a local club member who has given an interesting program to give it for the residents (remember, not just talking);
- bringing in a docile pet and building a program around it;
- asking a master gardener to make a presentation using real plants and flowers (many of this generation were gardeners themselves);
- starting lessons with a demonstration of something to capture residents' attention.

But the best medicine for stimulation is consistently showing up. Showing up on time every week builds relationship. Relationship is the foundation of intellectual, emotional, spiritual, and sometimes even physical stimulation. Even if lessons are mediocre, interrupted, or disjointed, it is the being present that speaks volumes.

More Suggestions

Allow time to look at materials. For example, looking at displayed quilts might take five to six minutes. Remember, if your display is large, it will take wheelchair-bound observers longer to maneuver around it. If you are passing around something small, be sensitive to residents' abilities; passing articles may be good therapy, or it may be impossible. If necessary, be prepared yourself to take an item around for viewing.

Plan extra material. I often plan too much and have something I could omit or use next time. I also allow extra time for the unexpected (a late start for some reason, medical interruptions, a person who needs to talk or be comforted).

A SAMPLE LESSON OUTLINE*

(Maximum total time: 40 minutes)

Introduction: In one sentence, outline the purpose of the lesson: *Since today is Mother's Day, we are going to look at some heart-warming stories about special mothers and sing a few hymns focusing on a parent's love.* (1 min.)

Involve residents personally: *What special memory do you have of your mother?* or *How did you show your children you loved them?* If there is little response, go on, allow "thinking time," and ask again later. (3 min.)

Short story: Share the history of a song that a mother wrote, inspired by her child: "God Will Take Care of You," by Civilla Martin. (10 min.)

*Appendix A on page 111 contains three sample lesson plans.

Sing: "God Will Take Care of You" (3 min.)

Main story, the day's topic: "The Patchwork Quilt," by Valerie Flournoy: A grandmother, mother, and daughter create family memories by quilting. Use photos, videos, real objects. Bring in some quilts; use anything that engages more senses than hearing. (10 min.)

Song: Choose a song that is thoughtful, slow. (3 min.)

Ask again for **their stories**. (3 minutes)

Short story: Give the history of the next song. (2 min.)

Sing: Choose a song that is lively. (3 min.)

Close: Summarize and suggest how to apply the day's topic. If appropriate for your group, a closing prayer would also be fine. (2 min.)

Teaming

It is very important to have a variety of support when providing lessons for a group in a care facility. Having a co-leader or a team brings more hands and more wisdom to any project. Volunteering can be draining if too much responsibility falls on just one person.

Let me elaborate. Preparing lessons requires time and energy, but when I first began, I did not have a larger view of where we might be a year from that time. I was fortunate that Priscilla, my co-leader, did. She worked directly with the facility's owner. She shared our vision, learned the facility's rules, and received permission for us to do what we wanted to do. Because Priscilla often visited her mother, she knew all the staff. She noticed if something had changed, if someone was absent, or if we needed to adjust our plan. During a lesson she could see who was tiring, who might need assistance, who was responding and to what, or who was singing for the first time. Afterwards we would discuss privately how a lesson went. I needed her feedback for future planning, and she helped me at times with preparation. Priscilla would run her new ideas past me as well.

Since personalities differ in any group, a variety of leadership personalities sparks more people's interest. Priscilla and I have quite different perspectives. I may have brought information and inspiration, but she added humor and insight. Her wit filled in my omissions and not a few awkward moments. We took turns encouraging each other when fatigue or distractions prevailed. Even though we started as good friends, we didn't always agree; working through differences deepened our relationship and mutual trust. Consequently, as a team we showed we were dependable, respectful, and committed to both residents and staff. We earned their trust.

For example, in the beginning we always allowed extra time to gather our attendees from their rooms. After about a year the staff began gathering them into our meeting room before we arrived. We cannot stress enough the gratitude we have for our facility's staff.

Their gentleness and optimism is contagious. We have come to depend on their perspective in many ways and never take their support for granted. After all, we have the same goal: making life as full as possible for the residents. A team mind-set is necessary and valuable for foresight, planning, and feedback.

The Beginning, Not the End

The end of our story is the beginning of yours. If you feel moved to action by our stories, you have fulfilled our best hopes for this book. It is our fervent desire to persuade you and empower you. Find a way in. Begin to love and honor your heritage by touching the hearts of the elderly near you.

III.

DEMENTIA
AND
ALZHEIMER'S
DISEASE

LYNETTE CRONER

DEMENTIA AND ALZHEIMER'S DISEASE

First Lessons

My experience with people with dementia has been growing for decades. It began when my grandmother exhibited the first signs of forgetting. I was given the privilege of seeing to her needs several times a year when my parents left town for vacation or short trips. Grandma was always very social and remained that way until she died in an assisted-living facility several years later. My last conversation with her was very pleasant, even though I had to explain to her who I was and how we were related. It was with my grandmother that I learned my first lesson about dealing with a person with a brain disease: The symptoms of the disease are not about me. The fact that my grandmother didn't know who I was did not detract from the wonderful time we had that day, or any other time we spent together. I was fortunate she was able to communicate her thoughts and memories so well. I learned to never become offended at another person's loss of memory. This was my opportunity to give love and compassion to a person who had loved and cared for me.

As time went on my aunt and then my mother were affected by dementia. Later my mother was diagnosed with Alzheimer's disease. The effects of her illness were more difficult for me. She eventually became in large part non-verbal. This is not to say she never spoke, but it was much less frequently. It also became more difficult for me to discern what she was saying when she did speak. When a designated caregiver placed her in a nursing home, I realized that there were a lot of people experiencing the symptoms of brain disease. As I spent time with my mom, I learned there still is much communication taking place with people who appear to be non-verbal.

The Challenge

One of the biggest challenges to encouraging a person with dementia or Alzheimer's disease is learning how to communicate. It is important to recognize that people with brain disease will have difficulty not only remembering things, but also thinking clearly, caring for themselves, communicating, and experiencing personality and mood changes. The more that I improved my own communication skills, the better prepared I was to interact with my mother and those living with her in the nursing home.

As time passed and the disease became more advanced, it took me longer to interact with my mom on any level. I had to be willing to take the extra time and attention necessary to communicate with her and the people living with her who were cognitively impaired. When the disease had progressed to the point that she was no longer as verbal, I still continued to talk to her about things that had always been important to her. I didn't always get a response, but many times I did. Through close observation of her body language, I knew she was understanding and appreciating my efforts.

I continued to mention the people my mom loved and to update her on their lives. We held hands while sitting together. I made it a practice to gently massage her back. In going about our daily routine, I got a fun response from her one day. I asked her if she would like her back rubbed, and she promptly sat up in her wheel chair so that I had access to her back. After that I celebrated every small communication she offered, verbal or not. She often responded readily to the offer of a back rub. Gentle touch communicates love and care.

Seven Things I Now Know

There are several important things I learned through caring for Mom and being around others with dementia and Alzheimer's disease at the nursing home.

1. When interacting with someone with brain disease, my attitude affects them.

I make it a point to always be respectful and to speak in a pleasant tone. The attitude I express through my tone when speaking to a confused person is as important as the words I use. I try to communicate openly and calmly through my body language. People see when I am nervous and reserved. I try to project a willingness to be present and caring. I always approach them from the front, because I may startle or upset a person if I approach or touch them from behind. When approaching an individual, I get their attention by calling them by name and identifying myself and purpose.

Just one note on addressing a person with any form of dementia: This is not the time in their lives to give them a new nickname. Some well-meaning individuals began to call my mother by a shortened version of her name. She had never been called by that name before, and it only confused her.

2. As brain disease advances, people become less verbal.

I learned not to mistake silence for a patient's lack of desire to interact with me. I found non-verbal cues can be effective in helping dementia patients to maintain focus. Examples of non-verbal cues include a touch to the hand or shoulder to remind the residents that I am there and listening. Or the cue might be a smile to let them know I enjoy spending time with them. I always speak on the residents' physical level. If they are seated, I lower myself so that they can see my face.

3. Speaking clearly and using simple terms seems to get the best results.

That means that I ask dementia or Alzheimer's patients only one question at a time. It is important to be patient when they are trying to speak. It may take time for them to find the words they're looking for. If someone with dementia is confused or doesn't understand, I try repeating my question or comment.

It can be confusing to residents if I try to rush a response. It can also be very counterproductive if I interrupt them or walk away before they finish what they have to say. I schedule my time so I don't feel rushed and can give the residents the time and attention they deserve. I pay close attention to their body language. For some, this may be their best form of communication. When I am supportive in my response, they seem to have more confidence in me and the friendship I offer them.

4. People with brain disease may be especially disoriented and confused when they wake up in the morning or from a nap.

At first this startled me, but I don't allow it to bother me anymore. Calmly help dementia sufferers begin to engage by directing them to something they enjoy. Mom was always the most engaged while we were walking together, or right after a walk.

5. The nature of brain disease may cause those who have it to act inappropriately according to common standards.

Elders with dementia do not have the ability to filter their thoughts and actions. With Mom, I tried to remind her what she should or should not do, but sometimes those attempts were useless. I tried to keep a sense of humor, never laughing at her, but acknowledging when I couldn't "fix" a situation.

There is no reason to feel embarrassed by an Alzheimer's patient's behavior. Mom liked to walk a lot. While walking around the nursing home, she often would approach more than one person she was sure she knew. In one such incident, she approached a woman who was seated in the lobby, took the woman's head in her hands, and kissed her right on the top of her head. The woman was very gracious and just smiled—I smiled back at her and wished her a good day. The incident was over in a matter of seconds. If I had tried to stop my mom, I would have only embarrassed everybody and made a big scene out of a small one. Besides, I found the whole thing quite sweet. After all, Mom was always a loving person.

6. It is not unusual for us to want to help people when they are taking a long time to complete a task.

It may take dementia patients a lot of time to do something as simple as combing their hair. However, it is important they be allowed to do as much as possible for themselves. Doing things for themselves is often a part of their occupational therapy. When someone took over a task Mom normally performed, she soon forgot how to do it herself.

7. It is helpful to obtain a life sketch of the patient from the family.

The sketch should include input from several people who know the person well. Because their short-term memory becomes impaired, dementia sufferers are more likely to talk about events that took place years before. If a caregiver, or even a grandchild, doesn't know about the people and events in the individual's life, communication can become stressful and frustrating for all. However, when armed with the life sketch, I can speak freely about those topics which interest the patient. If I find myself in a situation where a person is speaking about something of which I am uncertain, I just ask questions. Then they seem to enjoy telling me their thoughts.

Activities for Dementia/Alzheimer's Patients

Depending upon how far advanced the disease is, it can be difficult to stimulate a person with dementia. However, it is important that they be stimulated but not over-stimulated. With Mom, I found an activity as basic as folding towels was helpful. Simple games dementia patients already know and enjoy can be played. I had more success when I didn't try to teach new game rules or sequences. I was realistic in my expectations of Mom and tried to keep activities within her abilities. Enjoyment is the goal; don't worry about winning or losing. As I mentioned before, I use laughter when dealing with residents and am often a little silly. They may not understand my humor, but it communicates a fun and light-hearted atmosphere.

After watching responses from Mom and other people at the nursing home, I found that one activity that can be especially useful is music therapy. Listening to music that was popular when they were young adults is an enjoyable stimulating exercise for them. At the home Mom was in, musicians regularly volunteered to perform. I have been amazed at the response some of the residents have to music. One day my cousin was singing a silly song Mom had taught us as young children. Hearing the song, Mom got a big smile on her face and said in a joking tone, "Oh, not that one." We all knew the memories she had of pleasant times singing that song with us.

Music therapy can also be helpful when a resident is agitated. It has been shown that classical music may aid in restoring a sense of peacefulness to a person. Whether I was looking to stimulate or to soothe, I watched and listened for individual responses to particular pieces of music. I took note of those responses and let them guide my planning of future activities.

Often Mom would begin an activity with me but then become quickly distracted. Later she would sometimes wander back into the activity. I just accepted her distraction and, when possible, encouraged her to re-engage when she was ready. If, for example, we were in the middle of a movie, there was no need to re-start it. We just continued from where she had left off.

My goal in any activity is to make sure the people I'm attending feel cared for and included. A list of suggested activities and types of songs for people with dementia follows.

Examples of activities
- Walking—physical movement is very important.
- Reading or being read to. Watch for what is engaging to them.
- Playing cards—an easy game they already know; matching cards by number or suit, etc.
- Gardening—planting, weeding,

watering.
- Watching movies.
- Mixing ingredients in a recipe.
- Cooking.
- Going for a ride in the car through a familiar area.
- Looking through old photographs. Talking about them.
- Reminiscing.
- Recognizing colors.
- Performing light exercises—stretches.
- Making easy arts and crafts projects.
- Doing puzzles.
- Going out for a treat.

Examples of songs
- "You Are My Sunshine"
- "Take Me Out to the Ballgame"
- "Somewhere Over the Rainbow"
- "Blue Suede Shoes"
- "Amazing Grace"
- "This Little Light of Mine"

IV.
APPENDICES

———

A. THREE LESSONS PLANS
B. RESOURCES
C. HYMN AND SONG LIST
D. WORKS CITED

THREE LESSON PLANS

Because Internet sources are so quickly outdated, we chose not to include resource urls in the lesson plans. However, it is simple to make your own Internet searches by querying titles and the names of people or events that you're looking for. For instance, to find the words and chords to a suggested song, use the title of the song and the word "chords" as a query. Resource books used in the lessons should be available by request at your local library.

Lesson 1 (Inspirational)

Giving Out of What You Have
(Approximately 38 minutes)

Introduction: *Gratitude is today's theme. All our stories center around what happens when grateful people follow their hearts, which often leads to giving. Each story tells of giving out of what is in your hand at the time—not necessarily out of plenty, but maybe even out of poverty. Giving reflects the giver.* (2 min.)

Engagement: *Do you remember something special that was given to you? That you gave to others?* (3 min.)

Short story: Story about Alexander the Great in *One Simple Act*, by Debbie Macomber; a story about giving. (2 min.)

Song: *God's giving also reflects his heart, as shown in the story of this next song, "Now Thank We All Our God," by Martin Rinkart.* Share the history of the song found in *Then Sings My Soul*, Book I, by Robert Morgan. Show a picture of Martin Rinkart. (3 min.)

Main stories:

Read the North Platte Canteen story found in *One Simple Act*, by Debbie Macomber. *Sometimes one person's generosity multiplies. This is a story about a Nebraskan town that creates a train-station canteen for World War II GIs traveling to war.* (10 min.)

Read the 9-11 Delta 15/Canada story found on the Internet (query "Delta Flight 15 flight attendant story"). *Like the biblical story of God multiplying the little boy's loaves and fishes, this next story is amazing—and true. Several towns in Newfoundland, Canada, host an airliner rerouted and grounded due to the destruction of the World Trade Center Twin Towers on 9/11.* (5 min.)

Song: Sing "God is Still On the Throne." (3 min.)

Ask again for **their stories**. (3 min.)

Short story: Read "Phone Pianist" found in *One Simple Act*, by Debbie Macomber. A housebound pianist blesses others with her music. *God gave us what he had: his only Son, a* *reflection of God's incredible, generous, loving heart. Sending Jesus to earth to save us was a fulfillment of his promise to us. He is steadfast and always has us close in his heart; his words are true, sure, wonderful!* (2 min.)

Song: Sing "Wonderful Words of Life." (3 min.)

Close: Summarize and pray. (2 min.)

Lesson 2 (Scientific)

Never Quit
(Approximately 30-40 minutes)

Introduction: (Make this introduction specific to your own experience and situation.) *It always amazes me how people are gifted in an infinite number of ways. I just returned from visiting my New York family and was fascinated with my grandchildren's differences. One orders her own life and everyone else's around her; she's a budding administrator.* (Show pictures of grandchildren) *Another is drawn to animals and sees patterns in the physical world, creating amazing Lego block designs, each having a specific purpose; he's a budding scientist or engineer. The baby gathers beloved stuffed animals and brings them to each family member to hug and kiss; a budding veterinarian or social worker? So what is it that makes one person deathly afraid of spiders while another makes studying spiders his life's work? We each have been given gifts, eyes to see how they might be used, and a desire to see those inspired projects through.* (2 min.)

Song: Sing the hymn, "Open My Eyes That I May See," or the Disney song, "It's a Small World." (2 min.)

Main stories:

Read *My Brother Loved Snowflakes*, by Mary Bahr, and/or *Snowflake Bentley*, by Jacqueline Briggs Martin. *This is a story of a man who never gave up on his dream and who consequently gave the world a gift that no one had ever seen before.*

After reading, show the actual pictures of snowflakes that Bentley took. To find images on the Internet, query "snowflakes in photographs W.A. Bentley." (15 min.)

If you're able to give this lesson on a snowy day, bring in real snowflakes or ice on black paper and examine them with hand lenses. (5-10 min.)

What would happen in this world if we were all like Willie and never gave up on the dream and gifts put inside us? First of all, we'd be confident and trust, not in ourselves but in a power greater than ourselves. We'd trust in love and in the knowledge that there is a plan for us. Listen to this next inspiring story:

Show a picture of Fred Astaire. *After Fred Astaire's first screen test, the memo from the testing director of MGM, dated 1933, read, "Can't act. Can't sing. Slightly bald. Can dance a little." He kept that memo over the fireplace in his Beverly Hills home. Astaire once observed that, "...when you're experimenting, you have to try so many things before you choose what you want that you may go days getting nothing but exhaustion." And here is the reward for perseverance: "The higher up you go, the more mistakes you are allowed. Right at the top, if you make enough of them, it's considered to be your style."*

I don't know what quote you'd put over your fireplace, but I hope it can be said of all of us that "we'll try again tomorrow." Scripture agrees: "If we hope for what we do not see, we eagerly wait for it with perseverance" (Romans 8:25), and "...hope does not disappoint..." (Romans 5:5). Here are some other memorable quotes:

- *Winners never quit, and quitters never win.*—VINCE LOMBARDI

- *When you are going through hell, keep on going. Never, never, never give up.*—WINSTON CHURCHILL

- *If at first you don't succeed, try, try again.*—POPULAR ADAGE

- *Our greatest glory is not in never falling but in rising every time we fall.*—CONFUCIUS

And from the Bible again, God says:

- *I will not leave you nor forsake you.*—Joshua 1:5

- *Even to your old age, I am He, and even to gray hairs I will carry you! I have made, and I will bear; even I will carry, and will deliver you.*—Isaiah 46:4
(6 min.)

Song: Sing the hymn, "How Firm a Foundation," or "What a Wonderful World," by Louis Armstrong. (3 min.)

Close: *Mary Anne Radmacher said, "Courage doesn't always roar; sometimes it's the quiet voice at the end of the day whispering 'I will try again tomorrow.'" Let's end with that wonderful thought and face the coming week with courage.* (1 min.)

Lesson 3 (Spiritual)

Hope

(Approximately 27 minutes)

Introduction: *Every day we hear tragic stories on the news. Today I am bringing stories of hope to you. The longer I live, the hungrier I become for such stories. So let's begin with a hymn of hope.* (1 min.)

Song: Sing "God Will Take Care of You," in *Then Sings My Soul*, Book I, by Robert Morgan. (3 min.)

Story: *This is the story of Corrie ten Boom, a Dutch woman, who along with her family, was imprisoned by the Nazis for hiding Jews in their home. Regarding the horrific WWII concentration camps, one might ask, "Why?" We might ask the same today in the face of the senseless killings that have happened lately in our nation—"How do we forgive unspeakable evil?"*

But Corrie had a perspectve on forgiveness that is an inspiration to all.

Show pictures of the hiding place and Corrie ten Boom before and after WWII (query "Corrie ten Boom images" to find pictures online). *After Corrie's sister, Betsie, died in the Ravensbruk concentration camp, Corrie was freed through a fluke in the camp's bookkeeping system. She returned to Holland. In 1947 after the war, instead of letting bitterness and resentment take over her life, she began taking her story (and the gospel) anywhere she was invited. In today's true story, Corrie has returned to Germany to bring the message of God's love and forgiveness to that broken nation, and she's surprised by someone in the crowd, a previously feared concentration camp guard.* (2 min.)

Read from *One Simple Act*, by Debbie Macomber, of a former Nazi prison guard who asks Corrie ten Boom to forgive him. *Corrie forgave because she believed to do so was to be obedient to God. Was it easy? Hardly! But because of her obedience, she was given the power to forgive. God does not wish that any should perish. II Peter 3:9 says, "The Lord is not slow in keeping his promise, as some understand slowness. He is patient with you, not wanting anyone to perish, but everyone to come to repentance."*

Let this next song become the prayer of our heart, that our eyes may be opened to do God's will, too. (5 min.)

Song: Sing "Open My Eyes That I May See," from *Then Sings My Soul*, Book 2, by Robert Morgan. (3 min.)

Story: *My next story is about a Chinese woman God used to save abandoned babies. Her eyes were opened to help the helpless, and God supplied her needs.* (Query "Lou Xiaoying abandoned babies" for articles and images.)

China's controversial policy of birth planning instituted in 1987 has probably prevented more than 400 million births. Still there are, or were, many abandoned babies. Does God care? I believe he will use any means possible to save. Listen to the story of a remarkable woman in the Chinese city of Jinhua, in the eastern Zhejiang province, a city of 4.4 million (bigger than LA). Show pictures, read the story. (7 min.)

God cares for you, too! As we read this psalm

together, let the reality of God's care for each of us be revealed. Read Psalm 146: 1-2, 5-10. (1 min.)

Song: *Charles Wesley wrote this next song in 1744 after God rescued him from a mob that was destroying the church where he was preaching. He experienced firsthand the saving power of God as he was obedient to his calling.* Sing "Rejoice, the Lord is King!" from *Then Sings My Soul*, Book 2, by Robert Morgan. (3 min.)

Close: Summarize and pray. (2 min.)

RESOURCE LISTS

Finding reliable, interesting, free resources to support your activities with residents in assisted living is well worth the search. Below is a start. Following are lists of books and music, most of which are available from your local library or can be found on the Internet (which you can also use for free at most libraries). Given time, librarians can also locate and obtain books, CDs, and DVDs from other libraries if they do not have the item you requested on hand. When using material from the Internet, always be mindful of the authenticity of the source.

A. Stories and Books

Children's books (beautiful art and/or appropriate message)

Owl Moon, by Jane Yolen

The Patchwork Quilt, by Valerie Flournoy

The True Story of the Three Little Pigs, by Jon Scieszka

The Golden Egg Book, by Margaret Wise Brown

Georgie Finds a Grandpa, by Miriam Young (A Golden Book)

"The Ransom of Red Chief," by O'Henry

Five Minute's Peace, by Jill Murphy

Mr. Large in Charge, by Jill Murphy

The Jolly Postman or Other People's Letters, by Janet and Allan Ahlberg

The Velveteen Rabbit, by Margery Williams

The Night You Were Born, by Nancy Tillman

Snowflake Bentley, by Jacqueline Briggs Martin

My Brother Loved Snowflakes, by Mary Bahr

On Christmas Day in the Morning, by Pearl Buck

The Christmas Miracle of Jonathan Toomey, by Susan Wojciechowski

Sam and Poppy: A Dag of a Tale, by

Charles Nimmo

Shrek, the Famous Hermit Sheep of Tarras, by Tarras School students and teachers in New Zealand

Donavan's Word Jar, by Monalisa DeGross

Fidget's Folly, by Stacey Patterson and Vadim Gorbatov

Fidget's Freedom, by Stacey Patterson and Vadim Gorbatov

Fairy Tales

"Hansel and Gretel"

Aesop's *Fables*

Inspirational stories

Try querying the following on the Internet:

"North Platte Canteen" (small Nebraska town's train-stop canteen for GIs headed to war in the 1940s)

"9/11 Delta Flight 15" (Canada hosts Americans)

"Lou Xiaoying saving abandoned babies in China"

"Spokane ducklings rescue"

"Boy singing to his dying little sister"

"Amazing comeback from a fall in a race"

"Quotes on never giving up"

Inspirational Christian stories and lives

Try querying on the Internet,

"Anson Hui gifted young musician overcomes a genetic defect,"

and the following names:

Corrie ten Boom (survived German concentration camp in WWII)
Dietrich Bonhoeffer (courageous German pastor during WWII)
E.O. Sellers/Warner Sallman (teacher/artist)
Henry Van Dyke (inspirational life, writer)
Fannie Crosby (mission worker, poet, composer)
Philip Bliss (composer, choirmaster)
Charles Wesley (composer, poet)
Martin Luther (leader of the Protestant Reformation)
Isaac Watts (composer, theologian, logician)

Humor

Ogden Nash, any collection of his poems
She Who Laughs Lasts, by Ann Spangler
Never Sniff A Gift Fish, *A Fine and Pleasant Misery*, *The Grasshopper Trap*, by Patrick

McManus (especially good for those
who have hunted or fished, or come
from families that have)

Anthologies

The Bible
One Simple Act, by Debbie Macomber
One Perfect Word, by Debbie Macomber
He Shall Be Called, by Robert J. Morgan
Any *Chicken Soup* book
A Pioneer Sampler, by Barbara
  Greenwood
The Book of Virtues, by William Bennett

B. Music of 1940s Era

Internet searches using the following names
as key words will bring up hundreds of
songs, lyrics, and videos:

Glenn Miller Band
Tommy Dorsey Band
George Gershwin
Frank Sinatra
Louis Armstrong
Benny Goodman
Duke Ellington
The Mills Brothers
The Andrews Sisters
Fred Astaire

Judy Garland
Bing Crosby
Tex Williams

Hymn collections with stories

Then Sings My Soul, by Robert Morgan
Then Sings My Soul, Book 2, by Robert Morgan
Then Sings My Soul, Book 3, by Robert Morgan
Amazing Grace: 366 Inspiring Hymn Stories for Daily Devotions, by Kenneth W. Osbeck
The *Complete Book of Hymns: Inspiring Stories About 600 Hymns and Praise Songs,* by William J. and Ardythe Petersen

C. Community Resources

Library
Local historical society
Local newspaper
Residents' relatives

D. Visuals

Picture books

Norman Rockwell Poster Book, edited by Michael Schau

The Second Norman Rockwell Poster Book,
  introduction by Donald Holden
Raptors of the West, by Kate Davis
Snowflakes in Photographs, by W.A.
  Bentley
The Art of the Snowflake, by Kenneth
  Libbrecht
Family photos, residents' albums
Any artistic calendar

Short videos

Try making an Internet search for videos using keywords on the subject of your lesson. View the video from beginning to end before you use it to make sure it is appropriate for your audience.

Objects to enrich lesson topics

Wool, yarn, carding tools
Jar of interesting words
Feathers
Quilts
Rocks, minerals
Shells
Newspapers and magazines containing
  human interest stories and photos,
  especially those that are historical

E. Gifts

These can be purchased or hand-crafted and matched to lessons.

Snowflakes with inspirational quotes written on them

Cards—birthday, holiday, Thinking of You

Printed lists—quotes or Scriptures

Personalized notes appreciating the residents' laudable traits

F. Assignments

Gratitude list (include small spiral notebooks and pencils)

What have you done to pass on your legacy?

Recite together a favorite scripture, poem, or quote residents have learned by heart. Examples are Psalm 23 and The Lord's Prayer.

Think of a time you needed forgiveness. How did you handle it?

HYMN AND SONG LIST

Below is a short list of our residents' favorite music. Our group also enjoys and requests the stories behind these hymns (source books listed in Appendix B under "Hymn collections with stories").

A Mighty Fortress Is Our God, Martin Luther, 1529

All Hail the Power of Jesus' Name, Edward Peronnet, 1799

Amazing Grace, John Newton, 1772

America the Beautiful, Katherine Bates and Samuel Ward, 1910

Away In A Manger, author unknown, 1885

Because He Lives, William Gaither, 1971

Be Thou My Vision, Irish hymn, 8th Century

Blessed Assurance, Fanny Crosby, 1873

Christ the Lord Is Ris'n Today, Charles Wesley, 1739

Come Thou Almighty King, author unknown, 1757

Count Your Blessings, Johnson Oatman, 1897

Crown Him With Many Crowns, Matthew Bridges, 1851

Family of God, The, William Gaither, 1970

God Bless America, Irving Berlin, 1918

God Will Take Care of You, Civilla Martin, 1904

Great Is Thy Faithfulness, Thomas Chisolm, 1923

He Hideth My Soul, Fanny Crosby and William Kirkpatrick, 1890

He Leadeth Me, Joseph Gilmore, 1862

He Lives! Alfred Ackley, 1933

His Name Is Wonderful, Audry Mieir, 1959

Holy, Holy, Holy! Lord God Almighty, Reginald Heber, 1826

How Great Thou Art, Karl Boberg, 1885

I Am So Glad that Jesus Loves Me, Philip Bliss, 1870

I Love to Tell the Story, Katherine Hankey and W. G. Fischer, 1866

I Surrender All, Juddson VanDeVenter, 1896

In the Garden, C. Austin Miles, 1912

It Is No Secret, Stuart Hamblin, 1956

Jesus Loves Me, Anna Warner, 1860

Joy to the World, Isaac Watts, 1719

Joyful, Joyful We Adore Thee, Henry VanDyke, 1907

My Country 'Tis of Thee, Samuel Francis Smith, 1831

Nearer My God to Thee, Sarah Adams and Lowell
  Mason, 1840

O For a Thousand Tongues to Sing, Charles
  Wesley, 1739

Old Rugged Cross, The, George Bennard, 1913

Open My Eyes, That I May See, Clara Scott, 1895

Praise Ye the Lord, The Almighty, Joachim
  Neander, 1680

Rejoice, the Lord is King! Charles Wesley, 1744

Savior, Like a Shepherd Lead Us, Dorothy Thrupp
  and William Bradbury, 1836

Star Spangled Banner, The, Francis Scott Key,
  1814

This Is My Father's World, Maltbie Babcock, 1901

We Gather Together, Adrianus Valerius, 1597

What a Friend We Have in Jesus, Joseph Scriven
  and Charles Converse, 1855

Wonderful Words of Life, Philip Bliss, 1874

APPENDIX D

WORKS CITED

Sources for references on pages 78 and 79.

1. Bob Woods and others. Cochrane Dementia and Cognitive Improvement Group, "Cognitive Stimulation to Improve Cognitive Functioning in People with Dementia." Last modified February 15, 2012. Accessed July 24, 2013.
http://onlinelibrary.wiley.com/doi/10.1002/14651858.CD0055 62.pub2/abstract

2. The quote on page 78 is taken from http://www.mind-start.com/Research-Details_ep_45.html (accessed July 24, 2013). It refers to the following articles:

Dawn J. Brooker and Rosemary J. Woolley. Bradford Dementia Group, "Enriching Opportunities for People Living with Dementia: The Development of a Blueprint for a Sustainable Activity-based Model." Last modified June 25, 2007. Accessed July 24, 2013.
http://www.tandfonline.com/doi/abs/10.1080/1360786060096 3687?url_ver=Z39.88-2003&rfr_id=ori:rid:crossref.org&rfr_ dat=cr_pub%3Dpubmed&#preview

Brooker and Woolley found that "many practitioners in the dementia care field see activity and occupation as central to promoting well-being for people with dementia. Activities for people with dementia can be therapeutic, enhance quality of life, arrest mental decline, and generate and maintain self-esteem (Marshall & Hutchinson, 2001). Activities can also create immediate pleasure, re-establish dignity, provide meaningful tasks, restore roles, and enable friendships."

APPENDIX D: WORKS CITED

Betty Risteen Hasselkus. "The Meaning of Activity: Day Care for Persons With Alzheimer Disease." *The American Journal of Occupational Therapy* 46, no. 3 (1992): 199-206.
http://ajot.aotapress.net/content/46/3/199.full.pdf (accessed July 24, 2013).

Hasselkus reported that staff found "various purposes to the activity programming, including to provide pleasure, to keep the participants' minds alert, to promote bonding within the group, to provide physical exercise, and to help maintain the participants' skills. The need for flexibility was stressed..."

3. Alzheimer's Society. "Which activities are most engaging for people with dementia living in care homes?" *Research e-Journal* 11 (lay version).
http://www.alzheimers.org.uk/site/scripts/documents_info.php?documentID=1513&pageNumber=2 (accessed July 24, 2013).

"People with dementia need meaningful and enjoyable activities to live well. This can also help to reduce behavioural symptoms such as agitation, restlessness and aggression... Professor [Jiska] Cohen-Mansfield and colleagues have shown that simple activities such as conversation, personalised music or group participation in games are significantly more effective than 'care as usual' in improving the symptoms of agitation..."

PRISCILLA MARTENS is an Idaho native and resident. Her passions in life are preserving families, loving the elderly, and caring for odd and deformed animals.

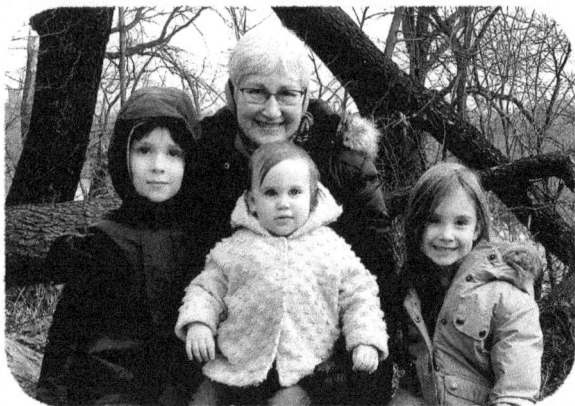

DEANNE RAMSEY is residing in southern Idaho, still following her passion for teaching, and traveling to see grandchildren as often as possible.

The authors can be contacted at:
lovingourheritage@gmail.com